With Jesus

Learning the unforced rhythms of His grace

By Marjie Schaefer

www.flourishthroughtheword.com

ISBN: 978-1-7328977-8-6

© 2024 by Marjie Schaefer. All rights reserved. No part of this document may be reproduced or transmitted in any form by any means, electronic, mechanical, photocopying, recording, or otherwise, without prior written permission of Marjie Schaefer.

Dedication

There is no way to quantify the influence a friend can have on your life.
There is an old saying that says,

"Show me your friends and I'll show you your future."

Vickie Adair

spent countless hours researching the hymn stories
provided for you in this study book.
She also put together the bibliography
and spent many hours proof-reading and editing.

Vickie, you are a worshipping warrior,
a trusted friend who is faithful, loving, fun, and available.
Thank you for your decades of friendship.

For your encouragement

*"Are you tired? Worn out? Burned out on religion. Come to me.
Get away with me and you'll recover your life.
I'll show you how to take a real rest.
Walk with me and work with me—watch how I do it.
<u>Learn the unforced rhythms of grace</u>." (Matthew 11:28 MSG)*

Jesus promised that as we came to Him, He would show us how to recover our lives and how to receive a real rest. He made it clear that we could learn the unforced rhythms of His grace. This is the aim of this study.

We can only learn these things as we come to Jesus and as we stay *with Him*.

Once we have knowledge, we have a tendency to make assumptions, but Jesus has made it clear that we still have much to learn. With Him as our master teacher, **learning beats knowing every time!**

With Jesus is a study that will take us all over the Bible. We will begin in the gospel of John, where we see Jesus exploding onto the earth and bringing grace and truth to humanity. From there, we will see how He interacted and taught His friends, the disciples, who ended up turning the world upside-down as they embraced the **rhythms** that He taught them.

> "When they saw the courage of Peter and John and realized that they were unschooled, ordinary men, they were astonished and they took note that these men had been *with Jesus*" (Acts 4:13 NIV).

With Jesus is a journey that will take us deeper into the Word of God. We will explore the reality of the Holy Spirit at work in our lives, and we will gain a clear picture of our truest identity in Christ. Throughout the study, tools are provided for you that are meant to equip you to examine the truth of the Bible and then make practical application in your daily life.

You will find that each chapter begins with a hymn. Hymns are theology set to music. Because we want to grow in our faith and in our biblical literacy, the hymns are provided as a tool for going deeper *with Jesus* in your worship of Him.

With Jesus contains five weeks of homework. Can you make the commitment to complete each day's study and come prepared to share your discoveries with your group?

Most of us do not hesitate to commit to doing our best at our jobs. Most of us have no problem being committed to our fitness programs, or keeping our hair appointments, or maintaining our volunteer positions to those causes we feel most deeply about. But can we make this same level of commitment to our Lord and Savior, Jesus Christ?

What would happen if we committed to be our very best in every area of our lives, including our personal Bible study?

Could we be like those early friends of Jesus who turned the world upside-down?

Let's not 'kinda try' to do it. Let's really do it. Ask the Lord to help you commit to bringing your best effort to this study over the next five weeks.

Jesus goes on to promise in Matthew 11:28:

> "I won't lay anything heavy or ill-fitting on you. Keep company *with me* and you'll learn to live freely and lightly."

Let's keep company *with Jesus!*

Every blessing,

Marjie

With Jesus
Week One

Blessed Assurance
Written by Frances J. Crosby
(March 24,1820 – Feb. 12,1915)

"Queen of Gospel Song Writers," Fanny Crosby's *Blessed Assurance* was published in Palmer's *Guide to Holiness and Revival Miscellany* magazine in 1873. Her dear friend, Phoebe P. Knapp, played the melody and asked Fanny what she thought. Fanny replied, "Blessed assurance, Jesus is mine."

Fanny wrote over 8,000 hymns during her lifetime. Blind shortly after birth, her family made sure she was educated, attending the New York Institution for the Blind (NYIB), and that she memorized five chapters of the Bible each week. Fanny said had it not been for her affliction she might not have been so well educated or developed an excellent memory.

"Although blinded by an illness at the age of six weeks, she never became bitter. One time a preacher sympathetically remarked, "I think it is a great pity that the Master did not give you sight when He showered so many other gifts upon you." She replied quickly, "Do you know that if at birth I had been able to make one petition, it would have been that I should be born blind?" "Why?" asked the surprised clergyman. "Because when I get to heaven, the first face that shall ever gladden my sight will be that of my Savior!"

At the time, very little money was paid for hymn lyrics ($1-2 per hymn). Fanny lived a very simple lifestyle giving away her extra money, and investing her time as a rescue mission worker. Fanny preferred to be known as a rescue worker than a hymn writer. Not only did she write hymns, but she also wrote political songs and patriotic songs for the Union during the Civil War. When asked about her hymn writing process she said she thought she was old-fashioned by going to the Lord in prayer asking for His inspiration. When Fanny died she asked that a small gravestone be erected saying, "Aunt Fanny: She hath done what she could; Fanny J. Crosby." However, May 1, 1955, a very large marble monument was erected by "friends to whom her life was an inspiration" which contains the first stanza of Blessed Assurance.

Blessed Assurance

Blessed assurance, Jesus is mine!
Oh, what a foretaste of glory divine!
Heir of salvation, purchase of God,
Born of His Spirit, washed in His blood.

Refrain:
This is my story, this is my song,
Praising my Savior all the day long;
This is my story, this is my song,
Praising my Savior all the day long.

Perfect submission, perfect delight,
Visions of rapture now burst on my sight;
Angels, descending, bring from above
Echoes of mercy, whispers of love.

Perfect submission, all is at rest,
I in my Savior am happy and blest,
Watching and waiting, looking above,
Filled with His goodness, lost in His love.

Week One, Day One
Who is this Jesus?

The disciple John wrote his gospel to provide Christians with a fuller understanding of the life and ministry of Jesus Christ. He wanted his readers to have a *settled faith* on the basis of the words and works of Jesus.

John wanted us to believe that Jesus is the Christ, the Son of God. The word **believe**—to trust; adhere to; rely on—occurs 98 times in the Gospel of John.

John knew through our belief in Jesus we would obtain eternal life. His purpose is actually stated in John 20:31 (Amplified):

> "But these are written, (recorded) in order that you may believe that Jesus is the Christ, (the Anointed One), the Son of God, and that through believing and cleaving to and trusting and relying upon Him you may have life through and (in) His Name (through Who He is)."

We begin our study in the Gospel of John, but we will journey throughout all of Scripture in order for us to have a *settled faith* and a strong belief in Jesus.

Read all of John Chapter One today and answer the following questions:

1. List out the four facts in verses 1-2:

2. Verses 3-5 are powerful verses. How do the words *life* and *light* describe the mission of Jesus, the Living Word?

3. What role did John, also known as John the Baptist (v. 6-8 and v. 19-32), play in this narrative. Why was this important? What did he call Jesus?

4. In verses 9-13, what do you learn about Jesus, the things He experienced, and what He gives to us?

5. John 1:14-18 is one of the most powerful passages in the Bible. Take some time to pause and reflect (*'Selah'*, the Bible calls this) on this section. Write out the top two things you glean from it.

6. Summarize your observations from verses 33-51.

Week One, Day Two
Jesus is the Word of God

If you did not complete yesterday's study, please take some time to do so now. John Chapter One is so foundational to our understanding of Who Jesus is and where we are going **with Him.**

Before you dive into today's questions, take a few minutes to worship Jesus by singing the hymn at the beginning of this chapter.

1. Read Genesis 1:1 and write out the verse. How does this verse 'jell' with the truth of John 1:2. How does John 17:5 confirm the opening words of John's gospel in verses 1-2?

2. John also wrote, through divine inspiration, the book of Revelation. In his vision, John sees Christ returning as a Warrior-Messiah-King. Read Revelation 19:11-13 and write out the title by which Jesus is called.

3. In your reading of Revelation 19:13, please note that the 'robe dipped in blood' that Christ wears is not the blood of His enemies, but rather **His atoning blood**. Show how Jesus reveals the character and purpose of God in each of the following verses.

    - John 1:1:

    - John 1:14:

    - John 1:18:

    - John 10:30:

    - John 14:9:

    - 1 John 1:1:

4. Read the following verses and write the specific way Jesus began His ministry:
   - Matthew 4:17:

   - Mark 1:15:

5. Based on 1 Peter 1:15-23, write out the reasons why you think Jesus began His ministry this way.

Week One, Day Three
We are created for relationship.

We've already studied John's (the Baptist) declaration of Jesus in John 1:29, "Behold! The Lamb of God who takes away the sin of the world!" Jesus came so that we could become 'children of God', as we believe in Him.

As we saw in the homework yesterday, He has made provision for us to be in relationship with Him through His atoning blood. That is, He died on the cross on our behalf, providing the perfect and complete sacrifice for our sins.

We are created for relationship with Jesus. Our obedience to Him, our dependence on Him, and our communion with Him, are all responses to His grace:

> *"For out of His fullness (abundance) we have all received (all had a share and we were all supplied with) one grace after another and spiritual blessing upon spiritual blessing and even favor upon favor and gift (heaped) upon gift."* (John 1:16 Amplified)

Our relationship with Jesus begins with repentance. Repentance means a true change of mind about sin and its cause. In this change of mind, there is also a change of heart, causing us to turn 180-degrees from sin and to God.

1. Read Romans 2:4 and write down what you learn about God and repentance.

2. Our salvation journey begins with an initial repentance. After that, our Christian lives are marked by God's grace and His goodness, which leads us to consistently repent (turn from) of anything that keeps us from God and fellowship with Him. Read the following Scriptures and list out what you learn about repentance.

    - 2 Timothy 2:25:

    - Acts 2:38:

    - Acts 5:31:

    - Acts 11:18:

3. Jesus calls His people to live in honesty and transparency with Himself and others. He equips and enables us to do this by giving us the gift of repentance. What is true repentance evidenced by, according to Acts 26:20?

4. Repentance is not a good work we do for God, but rather, it is one of the gifts of His grace to us. As we embrace the Person and work of Jesus Christ, we grow from a self-centered person to a Christ-centered follower. Jesus began His ministry with a call to repentance. Read the following verses in Revelation and write out His instructions to the churches:

    - Revelation 2:5, 21, 22:

    - Revelation 3:3, 19:

    - Why is Jesus cleansing the church, according to Ephesians 5:27?

    - What do you learn from 1 Peter 4:17?

5. We are declared *righteous* by the Lord at the moment of salvation, through the blood of Jesus Christ. *Holiness* is a daily walk of obedience, as we embrace the truth of God's Word, and live godly lives by the enabling power of the Holy Spirit. That being said, what do you learn about holiness from the following verses:

    - Hebrews 12:14:

    - 2 Corinthians 7:1:

    - 2 Timothy 2:21:

- 1 John 3:3:

- 1 Corinthians 6:18-20:

- Romans 12:1:

6. Repentance is not an easy subject to discuss or study; perhaps this is why we don't hear much preaching and teaching about it today. What does 2 Timothy 4:1-4 have to say about this very thing? Write down your findings.

7. The Word of God is our hope and our compass as we navigate these waters. What encouragement do you receive from 2 Chronicles 7:14?

8. As you wrap up today's lesson, take some time to do exactly what the verse above suggests; pray over the things you've studied today and any specifics for which the Holy Spirit has nudged you or pointed out in your own heart. Are there some things you need to repent of in your life right now? The best thing you can do is not put it off for another minute! Respond while this is fresh on your heart and while the Lord is speaking to you. Remember: repentance is a gift meant to lead us into deeper relationship with the Lord. He is not trying to punish you, but rather grow your relationship with Him.

Week One, Day Four
Revive us again!

So often we find ourselves in a gathering with other believers where prayers are being offered for revival. In the book *Prayer Portions*, author and teacher, Sylvia Gunter writes,

"Repentance is the forerunner of God's rains of revival."

1. Look up the following Scriptures and write out the phrases that reflect the cry and prayer of your heart.

    - Psalm 119:59:

    - Lamentations 3:40:

    - Psalm 85:6:

    - Psalm 80:18-19:

    - Habakkuk 3:2:

    - Hosea 6:1-3:

    - Hosea 14:4-5:

    - Proverbs 21:2:

2. What truth is communicated in Psalm 51:6-7. What does this mean for you in practical terms and day-to-day life?

3. Since transparency, honesty, truth, and holiness are the desires of God's heart for us, let's take some time to be still before Him and allow the Holy Spirit to point out anything in our lives that needs to be brought to the Lord and confessed. You have spent time looking up many Scriptures that speak of the mission of Jesus: holiness, repentance, and truth. Your mind has been renewed.

The following lists are provided as potential prompters for you to reflect on and ponder in your prayer time with the Lord. They are in no way meant to be for condemnation or accusation. You will know the Lord is speaking to you by the nature in which He speaks: Jesus is full of grace and truth (John 1:14). If present, He will point things out in your life that are specific. For example: *"You are still a bit angry at Susie Q for the way she snapped at you yesterday. Confess that and let Me have it."*

The enemy is the one who comes to you and says, *"You are a lousy Christian and you will never measure up; might as well just give up and be satisfied with the status quo."* Do you recognize the condemnation and accusation? That is not the way the Lord communicates.

Hudson Taylor, the great missionary to China in the 1800's, wrote, *"We are changed by beholding."* In other words, when we come face-to-face with our Holy God and His glory, we have two options: we can allow Him to change us by His loving grace and forgiveness, or we can run away from Him, and not deal with the things in our lives that need His touch.

Which option will you choose?

Use this list[1] today to reflect and pray. Take as much time as you need. This is between you and the Lord.

> *"Search me, O God, and know my heart; try me, and know my anxieties; and see if there is any wicked way in me, and lead me in the way everlasting"*
> *(Psalm 139:23-24).*

- Pride, refusing to humble yourself
- Selfishness
- Unforgiveness (Did anyone pop into your mind as you read this word?)
- Unbelief (fear, worry, hopelessness, anxiety, tension, living by feelings, what if?)
- Disobedience to God
- Refusing to hear God's voice of truth (have you turned away from God?)
- Holding on to sin (confessed but not repented of)
- Family disharmony/dishonor
- Esteeming money, homes, careers, people, cars over your affection for God
- Worry and anxiety—what is robbing your peace?
- Hypocrisy
- Judging others (see Isaiah 58:9; Matthew 7:1-5)
- Speaking wickedly of others
- Dishonoring the Holy Name of God (casually using His Name in conversation: "Oh My G__")
- Caring more about pleasing people than pleasing God
- Being unconcerned for people who do not know Jesus
- Gossip

---

[1] List taken from excerpts of *Prayer Portions*, by Sylvia Gunter, Repentance Section: pp. 8-10; 12-13; 30-33. Copyright 1991.

- Manipulation
- Gluttony/addiction to anything/your pleasure is your main priority
- Lying
- Pretense
- Deception
- Critical spirit
- Bitterness
- Resentment
- Impatience
- Keeping a record of your offenses
- Complaining
- Envy
- Jealousy
- Self-centeredness
- Self-pity
- Self-justification
- Concerned about defending your rights
- Unkindness
- Insensitivity
- Stubbornness
- Unloving attitude or actions
- Forsaking God
- Haughtiness
- Rebellion
- Impure thought life
- Strife
- Ingratitude
- Angry spirit
- Headstrong
- Unteachable
- Argumentative
- Stealing
- Defensive
- Harsh words

Week One, Day Five
Search my heart, Oh God!

Take the time today to review any verses that spoke to you over the course of your study time.

Sing or read the hymn at the beginning of this chapter.

You will be spending your homework time today reviewing the list from yesterday, as well as these questions provided for you below.

The reason we are doing this is because revival is deeply personal; it begins with us! If you were to write your name and draw a circle around it, revival and refreshment happens when everything in that circle is right with God.

Spend time prayerfully and reflectively allowing the Lord to speak to you from yesterday's list.

When you're ready, move on to these questions[2]:

- Is there anyone you have not forgiven?
- Is there anyone you are holding a grudge against?
- Is there anyone you hate?
- Have you allowed misunderstandings that you are not willing to forget?
- Is there anyone you dislike to hear praised or spoken well of?
- Do any of the following interfere with your relationship with God: your own plans, ambition, pleasures, loved ones, friendships, desire for recognition?
- Are you secretly pleased at the misfortunes of another?
- Are you annoyed over the accomplishments/advancements of others?
- Do you quarrel, argue, or get into heated discussions?
- Are there people whom you deliberately slight?
- Are you responsible for division in any relationships?
- Do you consistently overeat or drink too much?
- Do you have any habits that defile your body?
- Do you speak about the things you have done rather than what Christ has done?
- Have you made a pretense of being something you are not?
- Do you consistently feel you are not given enough credit?
- Are you self-conscious rather than Christ-conscious?
- Do you allow yourself to feel inferior to others?
- Do you do as little as possible in your work?
- Have you sought to evade paying your debts?
- Do you cheat or steal?
- Do you find fault with others on a regular basis?
- Are you consistently irritable and cranky?

---

[2] Questions taken from excerpts of *Prayer Portions*, by Sylvia Gunter, Repentance Section: pp. 8-10; 12-13; 30-33. Copyright 1991.

- Do you get angry and stay that way?
- Are you bitter towards God?
- Have you complained against God and the way He has moved and worked in your life?
- Do you tend to exaggerate and embellish stories?
- Do you carry prejudice against other Christians because they are a group that is different from yours?
- Do you allow impure sexual thoughts to linger in your mind?
- Are you given to lust or unclean entertainment?
- Do you find the Bible and prayer to be boring?
- Do you consistently stay away from church or meetings where the Word is proclaimed?
- Do you insist on having your own way most of the time?
- Do you find it hard to be corrected?
- Do you find that you are doing better spiritually than most other Christians?
- Is there rebellion towards one who wants to be restored to you?
- Are you more concerned about what people think than what is pleasing to God?
- Have you become influenced by the world?

These questions are not necessarily fun ones to work through. If you were nudged by the Holy Spirit on any of them, do two things:

1) If the sin/sinful attitude is against God, confess it and make things right with Him. 1 John 1:9 is called 'the Christian's bar of soap'. He forgives and restores as we confess.

2) If the sin/sinful attitude is against another person, confess it to the Lord, pray about next steps, and go get right with them if at all possible.

> ***"So, rend your heart, and not your garments;***
> ***return to the Lord your God,***
> ***for He is gracious and merciful, slow to anger, and of great kindness;***
> ***and He relents from doing harm"***
> (Joel 2:13).

Praying through this list, confessing and getting things right with the Lord and others is a beautiful example of 'rending your heart'.

Sin will take you farther than you want to go, keep you longer than you want to stay, and cost you more than you want to pay. ~Unknown

A Wheaton Story

In the opening college session in early 1950, a sermon was preached using 2 Chronicles 20:12 as the text,

*"O our God, will you not judge them?
For we have no power to face this vast army that is attacking us.
We do not know what to do, but our eyes are on you."*

The sermon stressed that sin clogs lives, and the preacher urged the audience to clean their lives of all that blocked God's power. Only a few students responded that day. Later that week, time was given for testimonies in another service. A respected professor on campus came forward to the microphone and publicly confessed that he was guilty of speaking unkindly to students about another faculty member. He then asked to be forgiven. The student body immediately came to life. This was something they had not seen before, and several students followed his example and confessed their sin.

As the week progressed, more and more students and faculty would take to the microphone each day at each service and would begin to name their sins publicly: cheating, pride, bitterness, resentment. At one point, the meeting was not dismissed and it continued throughout the night. Student after student, and faculty after faculty, would take to the floor to publicly confess their sin.

Spontaneous prayer and praise gatherings sprung up in many dormitories and houses as newly-forgiven students begin to attest to the Holy Spirit's transforming power.

An excerpt from a letter written at the time records the following:

"Last night I came home around 1:30am to go to bed, but I just sat fascinated listening to another student who was saved Thursday morning. He just sat there and it just kept bubbling out. He was in one of the groups of guys on campus who have been living terrible lives…breaking all the rules, stealing from the athletic department. He began digging out all of the equipment he had stolen out of his closet…."

Foreign and domestic newspapers quickly picked up the story, providing these headlines:[3]

"Students and Teachers Quit Classes in Non-Stop Prayer Meeting"
"Revival Meeting Reaches High Pitch"
"1,500 Students Pray All Night: Fervor Grips Wheaton Hall"

A report written gives this view as to what was happening:

"Some have wondered how we could be so long, thirty-nine hours in chapel. If you had been with us, you would have felt the presence and power of God. A newspaper man from Chicago who came to us, in his own words, 'with the cynicism of his trade,' remained to marvel at the earnestness and sincerity of the students. When one had met the Lord Jesus in reality, it did not seem long to wait six or eight hours to give one's testimony. A student from the University of Chicago heard what was transpiring at Wheaton and drove out to see what was happening. He sat in chapel form ten in the evening until three in the morning and then sought someone to help him find Jesus. A high school student passing the chapel at 11pm, felt drawn in, and was led to Christ."

---

3 "Revival at Wheaton", Published by International Awakening Press, Wheaton, Illinois, USA, 1994, by Mary Dorsett, pages 15-21.

Another student wrote,

> "I confess my stubborn and proud spirit didn't really enter into the spirit of the testimonies for a long while. I had not done some of the things that others said they had done. Wasn't I pretty good? Slowly I knew the Lord was speaking to me about things I ought to make right. I knew He wanted me to go the platform too, but I argued with Him and didn't want to give in. I knew I had a horrible attitude…..and had probably caused many to stumble. I knew I had criticized people. However, I wasn't quite willing to get up there in front of all those people…."

Later, this same student surrendered to the Spirit and spoke about how her pride and willfulness kept her from being totally devoted to Jesus.

The revival continued for over 10 days. It began with those who were already saved, seeking forgiveness, then followed with those who were not walking fully with Jesus, and then finally, those who were unsaved found their way to Wheaton from all over Chicago, and experienced salvation for the first time.

One student wrote, *"We all got right with God—when His search light showed us whether there were wicked ways in us….we all found we were just sinners saved by grace."*

Some lasting fruit from the revival of 1950:

- 38% of the class of 1950 devoted (at least) part of their lives to full-time Christian ministry.
- Three young men had a dream to establish a missionary radio station. They formed a non-profit organization, other students quickly joined with them. By 1952 the three men, along with their wives were in Africa, and missionary station ELWA went on the air in 1954. Before civil war rent the fabric of Liberia in the early 1990's, ELWA had five transmitters and broadcast the Gospel in 42 languages to Africa, Europe, the Middle East, and Russia.

With Jesus
Week Two

The Bible is the only book in the world that when you read it, the Author shows up.

Holy, Holy, Holy
Reginald Heber (1783-1826)

Reginald Heber was an English clergyman and hymn writer. During the last three years of his life he moved from England to serve as the Bishop of Calcutta, India. He died just short of his 43rd birthday. Reginald was the first to put together a hymnal around the church calendar. This hymn was for Trinity Sunday which is observed eight Sundays after Easter.

The four living creatures, each having six wings, were full of eyes around and within. And they do not rest day or night, saying:

"Holy, holy, holy,
Lord God Almighty,
Who was and is and is to come!"

Revelation 4:8

Holy, Holy, Holy

Holy, holy, holy! Lord God Almighty!
Early in the morning our song shall rise to Thee;
Holy, holy, holy, merciful and mighty!
God in three Persons, blessed Trinity!

Holy, holy, holy! All the saints adore Thee,
Casting down their golden crowns around the glassy sea;
Cherubim and seraphim falling down before Thee,
Who was, and is, and evermore shall be.

Holy, holy, holy! Though the darkness hide Thee,
Though the eye of sinful man Thy glory may not see;
Only Thou art holy; there is none beside Thee,
Perfect in power, in love, and purity.

Holy, holy, holy! Lord God Almighty!
All Thy works shall praise Thy Name, in earth, and sky, and sea;
Holy, holy, holy; merciful and mighty!
God in three Persons, blessed Trinity!

Week Two, Day One
Jesus is the Word

Last week as we studied, several names and descriptions of Jesus emerged, along with His mission and purpose. We will spend some concentrated time this week studying the Living Word and the importance of prioritizing it in our daily lives.

Jesus believed that living was ***initiated and sustained*** by God and therefore could not be measured by the physical senses alone. **Life is because God is.**

> "We literally exist by the power of God's Word. If He were to withdraw that Word, all life would utterly perish. This spiritual reality broadens our human responsibility significantly past the gratification of our own senses to encompass the honoring of God's Word that gives us life. If God's Word gives us life, how much more should we prioritize it on a daily basis?" ~ Author, Alicia Britt Chole

> "While people and churches around the world today have more access than ever to the Bible in their own language, I passionately believe people need to be given a much deeper understanding of Scripture, until their very blood is *'bibline'*—filled and flowing with the very essence of the truths of the Bible." ~Author and Theologian, John Stott

1. Read and write out Matthew 4:4 and answer the following questions:
   - What does this verse mean to you personally?

   - What was your first significant encounter with the Bible and what did God teach you through this encounter?

   - What are some things that nourish and sustain you spiritually? Write down and be prepared to share some of your spiritual habits that have helped you to know the Lord in real and relevant way.

2. Read Isaiah 43:10. Write out the difference between knowing, believing and understanding.

3. The great 19th century pastor, Charles Spurgeon said, *"A Bible which is falling apart usually belongs to someone who is not."* Look up the following Scriptures and write out the promises given to those who read God's Word:

- Joshua 1:8:

- Psalm 1:1-3:

- 1 Thessalonians 2:13:

- *"For the Word that God speaks is alive and full of power (making it active, operative, energizing, and effective); it is sharper than any two-edged sword, penetrating to the dividing line of the breath of life (soul) and (the immortal) spirit, and of joints and marrow (of the deepest parts of our nature), exposing and sifting and analyzing and judging the very thoughts and purposes of the heart"* (Hebrews 4:12 – Amplified).

Week Two, Day Two
Hear the Word

Hear the Word

1. Look up and write out Romans 10:17. What are some ways in which you are hearing the Word of God during this season in your life?

2. Read Luke 8:15 and write out two practical ways we can cultivate good soil in our hearts so that we bear good fruit.

3. In Proverbs 8:32-33, what does it mean to really hear, and what are the benefits?

Read the Word

4. Look up and write out Revelation 1:3. What do we receive by reading God's Word?

5. What is God teaching you about His character and nature as you read the Word in this season of your life?

6. Write down some practical ways that you can foster greater depth or variety in how you read the Bible. Come prepared to share these with your group.

Study and Memorize the Word

7. What do you learn about the Bereans in Acts 17:10-12?

8. Read and write out the highlights from Proverbs 2:1-5. What are the benefits of studying the Word?

9. Are there one or two more things that you would like to understand better in the Bible? What are they?

10. Read Psalm 119:9-11. Based on these verses, what can be a benefit of memorizing the Word? Think of a situation or time when you drew upon the Word that was embedded in your heart. How did the Word encourage or comfort you during this time?

Week Two, Days Three & Four

When Jesus walked the earth, the Gospels had not been recorded yet because He and His disciples were living them!

Peter, one of those disciples, had a spiritual journey that reveals to us how life can be transformed by knowing Jesus. Today, we know Jesus primarily through His Word. Peter knew the Lord face-to-face as the living, breathing Word. *"The Word became flesh and dwelt among us, and we beheld His glory..."* (John 1:14).

Jesus said to him in Matthew 16:18, *"Now I say to you that you are Peter (which means 'rock'), and upon this rock I will build my church, and all the powers of hell will not conquer it."*

Peter, the 'rock' on which Christ promised to build his church had an incredibly 'crumbly' start, but none of the disciples showed more growth in understanding both of self and of God during the three years of hanging out with Jesus.

1. Read about Peter's response to Jesus in Matthew 4:18-22. What do you think Peter *knew* about Jesus at this point in his life? Write down all of your observations about Peter from this passage.

2. Later in Matthew 14:22-33, Peter encountered Jesus walking on the water. Read this story. What do you think Peter *believed* about Jesus at this point?

3. Read John 13:5-17. What do you think Peter *understood* about Jesus through this incident?

4. Look in on Peter after his denial of Christ in John 18:15-27. Summarize how you think Peter may have been feeling after this.

5. What had Peter declared earlier in Mark 14:29?

Something to think about....

Later Peter would write two letters, the epistles of 1 and 2 Peter, and he would tell us this: "...*His divine power has given to us all things that pertain to life and godliness, through the knowledge of Him who called us...*" (2Peter 1:3).

What amazing encouragement for every believer. Peter had learned that experientially as he knew Jesus face-to-face.

> "The interweaving of the deepening knowledge of self and God that we have seen in Peter's experience illustrates the way genuine knowing of God and self occurs. Peter could not truly know Jesus apart from knowing of himself in relation to Jesus. He did not know himself until Jesus showed him who he was. But in learning about himself, he also came to truly know Jesus. Deep knowing of God and deep knowing of self always develop interactively. The result is the authentic transformation of the self that is at the core of Christian spirituality." ~David Benner, The Gift of Being Yourself

Week Two, Day Five

Spend your entire study time today in 2 Corinthians 4:5-15. Read the passage in several translations if possible (use *biblegateway.com* or the Bible app on your smart phone).

1. How did the word picture of being an earthen vessel holding a treasure impact you? What exactly is the treasure we hold, according to this passage?

2. What action step did Paul take in light of his own faith? (v. 13)

3. How can you apply this step in your own life? What would it look like?

4. Have you ever felt like Paul did in these verses? How has the Lord seen you through a troubled time recently? Write out a prayer of thanks to God. Finish your study time today by singing the hymn at the beginning of this chapter.

With Jesus
Week 3
Today always counts

Because He lives
By Bill and Gloria Gaither (~ 1970)

"A little while longer and the world will see Me no more, but you will see Me. Because I live, you will live also" John 14:19.

Husband and wife team, Bill and Gloria Gaither, have written over 700 songs together. The two would work together on an idea or concept for a song; Gloria usually writing the lyrics and Bill, the music. This hymn was birthed at a very difficult time in their life. America had been through the difficult 1960's with the increased drug culture, the sexual revolution, the Vietnam War, and the "God is dead" system of belief running through the educational system. Bill was physically weak from mononucleosis, and both he and Gloria, along with their church, had been falsely accused by someone they cared about. In Gloria's own words, she reflects on how the concept of this hymn developed:

"It was on New Year's Eve that I sat alone in the darkness and quiet of our living room, thinking about the world and our country and Bill's discouragement and the family problems—and about our baby yet unborn. Who in their right mind would bring a child into a world like this? I thought, "The world is so evil. Influences beyond our control are so strong. What will happen to this child?"

I can't quite explain what happened at that moment, but suddenly I felt released from it all. The panic that had begun to build inside was gently dispelled by a reassuring presence that engulfed my life and drew my attention.

Gradually, the fear left, and the joy began to return. I knew I could have that baby and face the future with optimism and trust. It was the Resurrection affirming itself in our lives once again. It was LIFE conquering death in the regularity of my day.

Because He Lives

God sent His Son, they called Him, Jesus;
He came to love, heal and forgive;
He lived and died to buy my pardon,
An empty grave is there to prove my Savior lives!

Chorus
Because He lives, I can face tomorrow,
Because He lives, all fear is gone;
Because I know He holds the future,
And life is worth the living,
Just because He lives!

How sweet to hold a newborn baby,
And feel the pride and joy he gives;
But greater still the calm assurance:
This child can face uncertain days because He Lives!

Chorus
Because He lives, I can face tomorrow,
Because He lives, all fear is gone;
Because I know He holds the future,
And life is worth the living,
Just because He lives!

And then one day, I'll cross the river,
I'll fight life's final war with pain;
And then, as death gives way to victory,
I'll see the lights of glory and I'll know He lives!

Chorus
Because He lives, I can face tomorrow,
Because He lives, all fear is gone;
Because I know He holds the future,
And life is worth the living,
Just because He lives!

Week Three, Day One
The Holy Spirit and us

> *"Grace is God's unrelenting commitment to deliver every resource we need to be what He's called us to be and to do what He's called us to do."*
> ~Author and teacher, Paul Tripp

As we continue our journey learning the *unforced rhythms of His grace,* this week we will see from the Bible that one of His grace gifts to us is the Holy Spirit. The Holy Spirit is that very resource spoken of in the quote above.

Have you ever thought of grace as God's *'unrelenting commitment'* to you?

Do you believe that you currently, today, have *'every resource'* you need to be what the Lord has called you be?

Let's begin this week by diving into John's gospel again in chapter 14.

Read John 14:15-31. Write down the specific things you glean in two areas: the things **Jesus says He will do** and **the Helper, the Holy Spirit.** Write your two lists in the space below and upon completion, pray over your findings.

Week Three, Day Two

In the Old Testament, the Holy Spirit is mentioned over 90 times, and in the New Testament, He is mentioned over 260 times.

The Holy Spirit is not a force, or a power, or an 'it'—the Holy Spirit is a Person.

1. From the following verses, write out how the Word shows us the personal qualities of the Holy Spirit:
   - Romans 8:27:

   - 1 Corinthians 12:11:

   - Romans 15:30:

2. What do you learn about the Holy Spirit from Isaiah 11:2?

3. Read Luke 11:9-13 along with John 7:37-39. Write down your conclusions about the Holy Spirit from these two passages.

4. From all of the verses you studied today, write out a prayer, expressing your heart and desires to the Lord in regards to the Holy Spirit. This is between you and the Lord only. Perhaps you didn't know much about the Holy Spirit before you started studying Him here in this chapter. Tell this to the Lord, and continue to allow Him to instruct you in the truth of His Word.

Week Three, Day Three

When God the Father hears and answers the prayers of Jesus to give us another Helper (John 14:16) in the form the Holy Spirit, He does so abundance.

1. Look up the following verses and write out everything you see and learn about the Holy Spirit:
   - John 3:34:

   - John 1:16:

   - Matthew 3:16:

   - Acts 2:33:

   - Ephesians 1:13:

   - Ephesians 3:19:

   - Romans 8:14-17:

2. As stated earlier this week, the Holy Spirit was active in the Old Testament as well. Look up the following verses and write down the specifics about the Spirit that are revealed in them:
   - Genesis 1:2:

   - Genesis 41:38:

   - Exodus 31:2-5:

   - Judges 3:9-10:

   - 1 Samuel 19:20-23:

   - Micah 3:8:

   - Ezekiel 36:25-29:

3. From your study so far today, review the things you have written down and write a summary paragraph of the truths you have learned about the Holy Spirit. In other words, if you had to explain the Presence of the Holy Spirit to a genuinely curious inquisitor, what would you say to him or her?

Week Three, Day Four

The Holy Spirit is very active in drawing us into a saving relationship with Jesus Christ, and then He keeps our relationship with Jesus active, alive, fresh, and powerful.

1. Look up the following verses and write down the specific actions of the Holy Spirit in our salvation:
   - John 16:5-15:

   - Titus 3:5:

   - 2 Thessalonians 2:13:

   - John 14:17:

   - Romans 8:9-11:

Take the time to pray and do two things right now. If you have never yielded your life to Jesus in a saving relationship and are discovering this through your current study of the Bible, ask Him now to come and be your Savior. Confess to Him the sin in your heart and life that has kept you from knowing Him and following Him as Lord. Yield the control of your life to Him and ask Him to take over. You never lose by believing God. This is the most important decision you make in your entire life.

If you have known the Lord for some time, thank Him for being your Lord and Savior and for giving you the precious gift of the Holy Spirit. Ask Him to refresh your relationship and renew you in the power and strength of the Holy Spirit. Ask Him to fill you in new and fresh ways and to continue to open your eyes to the wonder of His salvation and His glory and grace!

2. The New Testament gives us a beautiful picture of the work of the Holy Spirit in our lives. The Bible reveals the personal acts of the Holy Spirit. Look up these verses and write down what you discover:
   - Matthew 4:1:

   - Matthew 10:20:

   - John 14:26:

- John 16:8-11, 13:

- Acts 1:8:

- Acts 2:4:

- Acts 13:2:

- Romans 5:5:

- Romans 8:26:

- 1 Corinthians 2:10, 13-15:

- Ephesians 3:16:

- Revelation 2:7:

Week Three, Day Five
Walking in the Spirit

One of the goals of this Bible study is to equip you with tools to study the Bible on your own, without the weekly accountability of a book study and group meeting. Participating with a community of women who are committed to digging into God's Word is another aspect of God's grace to us! Having the freedom to gather together, worship, pray and then hear what we've learned from one another is not to be taken lightly. We praise God for this season to be together!

Here is a potential tool for your ongoing study in God's Word.

Please use the <u>devotional method</u> to study Galatians 5:16-25.
- Pray for insight as you read the passage and ask for direction on how to apply it.
- Take some time to meditate (think deeply about it; focus your mind for a period of time in silence) on the verses that jump out at you and really speak to you.
- Write out an application for those verses; personalize this for you.
- Memorize a key verse from your study.

Come prepared to share your results with your group.

With Jesus
Week Four

Jesus loves us

Jesus Paid It All
By Elvina M. Hall, 1865

During a sermon, while in the choir loft at Monument Street Methodist Church in Baltimore, Maryland, Elvina penned the words to this hymn. The only trouble was, she didn't have paper, so she wrote the lyrics as they came to her on the flyleaf of her hymn book. At the same church, the choir director, John Thomas Grape, had just handed the pastor a new tune he had written. When Elvina gave her lyrics to that same pastor, he quickly realized that the tune and lyrics would marry nicely. The new hymn was published in the periodical *Sabbath Carols*, and it quickly became an American favorite.

Jesus Paid it All

I hear the Savior say,
"Thy strength indeed is small;
Child of weakness, watch and pray,
Find in Me thine all in all."

Refrain:
Jesus paid it all,
All to Him I owe;
Sin had left a crimson stain,
He washed it white as snow.

For nothing good have I
Whereby Thy grace to claim;
I'll wash my garments white
In the blood of Calv'ry's Lamb.

And now complete in Him,
My robe, His righteousness,
Close sheltered 'neath His side,
I am divinely blest.

Lord, now indeed I find
Thy pow'r, and Thine alone,
Can change the leper's spots
And melt the heart of stone.

When from my dying bed
My ransomed soul shall rise,
"Jesus died my soul to save,"
Shall rend the vaulted skies.

And when before the throne
I stand in Him complete,
I'll lay my trophies down,
All down at Jesus' feet.

Week Four, Day One
Jesus loves us

1. Read John 17:20-26 in several translations. Write out the verses or phrases that really speak to you from the prayer of Jesus.

2. What kind of difference does it make in your life knowing that Jesus has prayed for you and does pray for you? Give specifics.

3. How does this prayer of Jesus for you and other believers, including His own disciples, spur you on in your own prayer life? How is praying for someone an act of love?

4. Spend the rest of your time today praying for the loved ones in your life. Use the prayer of Jesus in this passage as a guide to pray for them. Make sure you include praying for the church (your own and the church worldwide) and asking the Lord to continue to make us one so the world will believe that Jesus is Lord!

Week Four, Day Two

Read John 17:20-26 again.

1. Verse 21 reveals two priorities of Jesus. What are they? Why do you think (from your study so far through *With Jesus*) these two priorities are so important to Jesus?

2. How does John 13:34-35 confirm Jesus' two priorities?

3. In John 17:22, Jesus comments on the glory He has given to us, His disciples. Look up 1 John 1:3 and 2 Corinthians 3:18 and tie in these verses with the glory Jesus declares in John 17.

4. Use the devotional method again on this passage in John 17:

- Pray for insight as you read the passage and ask for direction on how to apply it.
- Take some time to meditate (think deeply about it; focus your mind for a period of time in silence) on the verses that jump out at you and really speak to you.
- Write out an application for those verses; personalize this for you.
- Memorize a key verse from your study.

Come prepared to share your results with your group.

Week Four, Day Three

In His final prayer, Jesus prays for the unity of all believers throughout all generations. This oneness He prays about is not an organizational unity, but rather a spiritual unity which can be visibly obvious to the watching world as it is manifested in the church.

Read John 17:20-26 again today.

1. Verse 23 is a revealing verse in this section of the passage, as it shows us the key to our victorious life in Christ. What is that key?

2. There is a pattern of unity that characterizes the relationship of the Father and the Son, and the Son and the believer. Using the chart provided for you below, fill in the categories with verses from John 17 that reveal the different aspects. You will need to read *all* of John 17:1-26. The first one is done for you:

	Father to Son	**Son to Believer**
Unity	v. 21, 20	v. 21, 23, 26
Glory		
Love		
Mission		
Knowledge		

Week Four, Day Four

We have already seen amazing and profound truths from the Word of God as we continue on our journey *With Jesus.*

The beauty of being united with the Son of God is that we know Jesus is not only **with us,** but He is also *in us* through the power and presence of the Holy Spirit.

We are called to share in what He is doing. We are equipped to pray as He did in John 17, on behalf of the church and those who do not believe in Him yet. We are called to share in the love the Father has for His Son.

Praise God for His love for us through Jesus the Son! Go back through your study book and spend a few minutes singing through your favorite hymn (or all of them!) as an act of worship.

1. Today you will be doing an abbreviated version of a chapter analysis Bible study.

    - Read though all of Romans Chapter 8 one time. Read it a second time and underline the phrases or words that speak to you and resonate with you.
    - On your third time through, list out the specific benefits of Jesus who is with you and in you. You should find at least 18 things from this chapter.
    - The first one is done for you.

    I am not condemned. (Romans 8:1)

Week Four, Day Five

Take the time today to complete any of the homework from this week that remains unfinished.

From your chapter analysis work in Romans 8 yesterday, please do some additional study on it by following these instructions:

1. Write out a chapter summary of what you learned from your study. This could be one or two paragraphs, but make it as succinct as possible:

2. List any questions that came up for you in your study of Romans 8.

3. Find any additional passages that correlate with Romans 8 by looking up any cross-references provided for you in your Bible. List the references here:

4. Write one personal application from your study of Romans 8.

With Jesus
Week Five

Trust and Obey for there's no other way……

Trust and Obey
By John H. Sammis, 1887

John Sammis was called by God to leave his business career and attend seminary. He was ordained as a Presbyterian pastor in 1880, served at several churches, then joined the faculty of the Los Angeles Bible Institute.

The hymn was inspired in 1886 when the composer of the music, Daniel B. Towner (1850-1919), was the music leader during one of Dwight L. Moody's famous revivals. Towner provided the following account cited by Moody's musical partner, Ira D. Sankey, in his biography, My Life and the Story of the Gospel Hymns:

"Mr. Moody was conducting a series of meetings in Brockton, Massachusetts, and I had the pleasure of singing for him there. One night a young man rose in a testimony meeting and said, 'I am not quite sure—but I am going to trust, and I am going to obey.' I just jotted that sentence down and sent it with a little story to the Rev. J. H. Sammis, a Presbyterian minister. He wrote the hymn, and the tune was born."

Trust and Obey

When we walk with the Lord in the light of His Word,
What a glory He sheds on our way!
While we do His good will, He abides with us still,
And with all who will trust and obey.

Refrain:
Trust and obey, for there's no other way
To be happy in Jesus, but to trust and obey.

Not a shadow can rise, not a cloud in the skies,
But His smile quickly drives it away;
Not a doubt or a fear, not a sigh or a tear,
Can abide while we trust and obey.

Not a burden we bear, not a sorrow we share,
But our toil He doth richly repay;
Not a grief or a loss, not a frown or a cross,
But is blessed if we trust and obey.

But we never can prove the delights of His love
Until all on the altar we lay;
For the favor He shows, for the joy He bestows,
Are for them who will trust and obey.

Then in fellowship sweet we will sit at His feet,
Or we'll walk by His side in the way;
What He says we will do, where He sends we will go;
Never fear, only trust and obey.

Week Five, Day One
Becoming a disciple with Jesus

Spend some time singing through the hymns today.

The last thing Jesus said to all of His friends before He ascended to heaven after the resurrection was, *"Therefore go and **make disciples** of all nations, baptizing them in the name of the Father and of the Son and of the Holy Spirit, and teaching them to obey everything I have commanded you. And surely I am with you always, to the very end of the age"* (Matthew 28:19-20).

Being a disciple of Jesus Christ means so much more than just being a *believer in* Him or a follower of Him. There is a marked difference between being a believer and being a disciple.

Being a disciple is more than just going to church once or twice a week (or month). Enjoying Christian fellowship with your friends is a delightful part of the Christian life, but that in and of itself is not discipleship.

The goal of this time together in our study **With Jesus**, has been to deepen our understanding and application of what it means to be a disciple of Jesus.

Discipleship is a process in which we ***intentionally develop progressively*** in our spiritual maturity so that we will be able to share with others what we know to be true of Christ. This is called life-upon-life ministry, or spiritual reproduction.

One of the main goals of discipleship is to fulfill what Jesus commissioned us to do in His last instructions before leaving earth: live life with Jesus as our Lord, and then help others to do the same.

Our highest calling and purpose is to disciple others—in our relationships at home, at work, at church, through mentoring, or in a variety of ways—our lives are meant to be centered on the eternal purposes of Jesus: knowing Him intimately and making Him known to others.

One of the main components of growing in our own spiritual maturity is knowing who we are in Christ.

1. Read Galatians 4:4-7. Use the verse-by-verse analysis method:
   - Write out all the facts of this passage.

   - Write the verses in your own personal paraphrase.

   - Write out your applications/insights from the passage.

2. What was God's purpose in sending Christ, according to this passage. How does God assure our 'sonship' and how are we able to call out to God?

Week Five, Day Two
Walking with Jesus

"It's in Christ that we find out who we are and what we are living for" (Ephesians 1:11 MSG).

Another way of saying that is, *"Jesus Christ's work of redemption is the centerpiece of all history on earth and in heaven."* ~Jean Fleming, Pursue the Intentional Life

1. Read Colossians 2:6-10. How did you personally receive Christ? Write out your testimony in five sentences or less.

2. What does it mean to 'walk in him' (v. 6)? How are you doing that each day?

3. What do you think it means to be rooted and built up, established in the faith like verse 7 tells us? Would you say that these three terms describe your journey with Jesus? If not, spend some time talking with Him about this and pray about how you can begin to develop a deeper 'root system'.

4. How is it possible for a believer of Jesus to be cheated through philosophy (v. 8)?

5. What do you think are some 'traditions of men' that we are exposed to today? How do they impact our walks with Jesus?

6. Verses 9-10 are an amazing statement of truth for each believer in Jesus. How do these truths impact your daily life? Complete today's study by writing a prayer of gratitude to God based on these verses.

Week Five, Day Three
The Word of God addresses speaking what is true

1. Read and write out 2 Corinthians 4:13.

2. What are the two verbs in this verse?

3. Paul is quoting Psalm 116:10. Write it out here:

4. Do a word study on **believe** and **speak**; follow these easy steps:
    - Write the English definition from the dictionary.
    - Look up different translations of the verse and compare the wording of each one.
    - Look up the Greek or Hebrew word or the root word if possible. (Try an online Greek New Testament or Greek Lexicon.)
    - Write out the insights you glean from your study.

5. Look up each of the Scriptures listed here. Next to each one, write the word or words that relate to speaking:

   - Proverbs 18:21:

   - Matthew 12:37:

   - Romans 4:17:

   - Romans 8:31:

   - Romans 10:8-11:

Week Five, Days Four & Five

As we wrap up our five weeks together through this study, my prayer is that you have seen how deep and how wide is the Word of God! We cannot plumb its depths. From your time spent in the Scriptures yesterday, I hope you realized in a fresh way, how important it is to speak what we believe to be true. Even the great Apostle Paul, the man we think of who had such great faith, made it a habit to 'believe and speak'. The Bible tells us that faith comes by hearing and hearing by the Word of God (Romans 10:17).

One of the best ways for our faith to grow is for our own ears to hear our own mouths speaking the truth of the Word of God **out loud.**

For the next two days and for any time remaining before you begin another study, take a few verses a day and write out your own personal identity and declaration statement based on the Word of God.

Use the verses provided for you to get started. Be sure and take the time to believe and therefore speak!

Philippians 4:13	Romans 6:6, 11	John 14:1, 27
2 Corinthians 9:8	2 Timothy 4:18	Romans 9:23
Romans 15:7	Colossians 3:3	Ephesians 1:11
Galatians 2:20	1 Corinthians 1:5	1 John 5:4-5
1 John 2:27	Philemon 6	Philippians 1:7
John 17:9	Philippians 1:11	James 1:2-4
1 Thess. 5:23	Galatians 5:22-23	Matthew 6:33
Ephesians 1:3	Colossians 1:9	Romans 1:7
1 John 5:18	Romans 8:2,18,28	2 Timothy 2:3-4
Romans 6:4	Romans 12:6	Romans 6:22
1 Corinthians 1:9	Romans 5:2	Ephesians 4:1
Ephesians 5:29	Ephesians 1:4	2 Corinthians 2:14-15
John 15:3	1 Corinthians 11:7	1 Corinthians 3:16
Galatians 3:27	1 Peter 1:23	Matthew 6:26
Romans 8:37	1 Corinthians 6:11	Colossians 2:3
Ephesians 2:10	Hebrews 13:5	

How to have a meaningful daily quiet time

Attitude is everything:
- Come to God with a sense of expectancy and an eagerness to hear from Him.
- Come into His Presence with reverence.
- Ask Him to give you a willingness to obey Him, no matter how He leads you.

Select a specific time:
- Choose the time to read and pray when you are at your best.
- Give God your time and attention.
- Be consistent with the time you set to meet with God.
- If you've not been consistent in the past, start with **seven minutes**. Everyone can spend seven minutes.

Follow a simple plan that works for you:
- *If you aim at nothing, you will surely hit it.* Have a meaningful plan in place; key word: plan.
- *Relax:* 'Be still and know that He is God.' (Ps. 46:20). Quiet yourself before Him.
- *Request:* Pray briefly and ask Him to speak to you: "Search me, O God"; "Open my eyes to see wonderful things in your Word." (Ps. 139:23; Ps. 119:18)
- *Read:* This is where your conversation with God begins. He speaks to you through His Word.
- *Reflect:* Don't rush; meditate on the Scriptures you have read. Journal what you have gleaned.
- *Request:* After the Lord has spoken to you through His Word, speak to Him in prayer, asking according to things He has revealed.

A simple acrostic to aid in your prayer time:
- **P-Praise the Lord.** Praise God for Who He is; thank Him for His blessings.
- **R-Repent of your sins.** Confess and ask Him to help you turn away from any revealed sin.
- **A-Ask for yourself and others.** Pour out your heart to God in prayer.
- **Y-Yield to God's will.** Reaffirm the Lordship of Jesus Christ in your life, along with your willingness to trust and obey Him.

Your main purpose in having a daily quiet time with the Lord is to get to know Him and to hear from Him. This is not a ritual but a <u>relationship</u> with the living Lord.

A simple suggestion:
- Read the Psalm of the day and every 30th Psalm, completing the entire book of Psalms in one month: Psalm 5, 35, 65, 95, 125.

Works Cited

The Amplified Bible. Grand Rapids, MI: Zondervan Bible, 1983. Print.

Benner, David G. *The Gift of Being Yourself: The Sacred Call to Self-discovery*. Downers Grove, IL: InterVarsity, 2004. Print.

Chole, Alicia Britt. Anonymous. Nashville: Integrity, 2006. Print.

"Fanny Crosby Biographies." Fanny Crosby Biographies. N.p., n.d. Web. 21 Aug. 2015.

Fleming, Jean. Pursue the Intentional Life: Teach Us to Number Our Days, That We May Gain a Heart of Wisdom (Psalm 90:12). N.p.: n.p., n.d. Print.

Gaither, Gloria. "Amazing Hymn Stories | TanBible.com." Amazing Hymn Stories | TanBible.com. N.p., n.d. Web. 21 Aug. 2015.

Gunter, Sylvia. Prayer Portions. Birmingham: Father's Business, 1995. Print.

Hawn, C. Michael. "History of Hymns: "Trust and Obey"" Discipleship Ministries The United Methodist Church, n.d. Web. 23 Aug. 2015.

Holy Bible: New International Version. Grand Rapids, MI: Zondervan, 2005. Print.

Peterson, Eugene H. The Message. Colorado Springs, CO: NavPress, 2004. Print.

About the Author

Marjie Schaefer was born in Georgia, raised in Texas, and has spent the past four decades in Washington State. She and her husband, Steve, have been married for 36 years and have four grown children and two grandchildren.

Marjie describes herself as an everyday girl who loves Jesus and daily pursues a life with Him at the center of her activities and purposes.

She started leading and teaching Bible studies while a student at Washington State University and has continued to open her home and her life to anyone who wants more of the Word and more of Jesus. Her greatest passion is bringing the Word of God to life through practical application and visual tools. Women look forward to her personal touches while attending her studies, and they usually go home with tangible reminders of God's love for them.

Marjie started spending deliberate and daily time in the Word of God while she was a young girl at the encouragement of her godly mother. This has given her a foundation that has stood the test of time. She began writing her own Bible studies at the request of some friends who desired to study the Word during the summer months.

Marjie and her team currently lead the ministry, **Flourish Through the Word,** a 501c3 organization which is a community of women in the greater Seattle region committed to being equipped through God's Word. As a result of their time together in the Word, the women move out into their arenas of influence, shining their light for Jesus. You can find out more about this ministry, upcoming events and Bible studies at www.flourishthroughtheword.com.

Cover Artwork Design…..

Cheryl Westrom

Cheryl leads a Flourish group in California. Marjie asked her to design and create the cover art for this study. Here are her words describing the process:

When Marjie asked me to create a piece of artwork for this Bible study, I was both honored and terrified! I was pretty sure I wasn't ready for the task, but both Marjie and the Lord had more confidence in my skills, so I said yes.

I have loved this passage of Scripture for many years. As I meditated on the words, 'walk with Me, watch how I do it, learn the unforced rhythms of grace', I kept coming back to that phrase: unforced rhythms.

When I would get away with my family to the lake and was in the boat and felt the unforced rhythms of the water, it made me think of Jesus and His word to His people. This is what I wanted to capture in this piece.

I looked up a photo of the Sea of Galilee, olive trees, and what fishing boat from back in the days of the disciples might look like. From those inspirations, I created this design.

The boat is made with wood from the apple tree we cut down in the backyard. The frame is made from fence boards that needed replacing. The actual sand is from Cuba, brought back from my daughter's trip there in 2018.

I enjoy creating, and while I'm new to the art from, I'm excited to see how God is going to use it in my life to bring others closer to Him.

www.ingramcontent.com/pod-product-compliance
Lightning Source LLC
Chambersburg PA
CBHW082214070526
44585CB00020B/2407